Seven
Overcomin

Titles in the Christian Counselling Series

Seven Steps to Overcoming Depression

Selwyn Hughes

Marshalls

Marshalls Paperbacks
Marshall Morgan & Scott
1 Bath Street, London EC1V 9LB

First published by Marshall Morgan & Scott 1982

ISBN 0 551 00949 7

Printed in Great Britain by
Richard Clay (The Chaucer Press) Ltd,
Bungay, Suffolk

Contents

Preface

The books in the *Christian Counselling Series* are written with two main groups of people in mind. The first group are those who facing a personal problem look for something concise and readable that speaks to their need. The second group are ministers and counsellors who wish to place in the hands of people seeking help something that will supplement their own individual counselling efforts.

The authors, writing from their own personal encounters with people who have faced the problems listed in this series, do so with a good deal of confidence. They claim that when the principles outlined in these books have been followed they have contributed in a positive manner to helping people resolve their difficulties. The content is firmly based on Scripture, but the authors in their writing seek to apply Biblical principles in such a way that helps readers, not only to know what they should do but how to do it.

Introduction

Carol sat in the corner of the counselling room look-ing thoroughly downcast and dejected. 'How can I help you, Carol?' I said, taking a seat opposite her. It was a full three or four minutes before she spoke. 'I wish I could die,' she began. 'For weeks now I have suffered this awful feeling of blackness and despair. When I awake in the morning, I have no desire to get out of bed, and all I feel like doing is pulling the blankets over my head and hiding away from the world. I've seen my doctor about it, but the tablets he has given don't seem to be a great help. I've talked to my minister about it, and though he has helped me a little, I still can't seem to shake it off. I've been praying that you might be able to help me, and this is why I've come.' Her tone suggested that I might be her last hope.

'Tell me a little more about how you feel, Carol' I said, 'and take your time because, before trying to help you with your problem, I want to understand it as best I can.' Carol then burst into tears, and after a few minutes of deep sobbing, said, 'It seems I have a steel band around my head that gets tighter and tighter every day. Nothing I do seems to be able to break it. I've tried praying and reading the Bible, but even this seems to get me nowhere. My hus-band and children are suffering because of it. My house is in a mess because I haven't done any housework for weeks. Life is just not worth living.'

Carol was suffering from Britain's number one problem – depression. As a counsellor, I see more people afflicted by depression than by all other emotional problems put together. It took several sessions of counselling before Carol was able to cope with her depression, but after a few weeks, implementing the principles and insights I shared with her, she was able to manage her home and care for her family without too much difficulty. In two months, she was fully recovered. Some of the insights I shared with Carol, I would like to share with you in these pages, in the hope that they might help you, as they have helped others, climb out of the dark pit of depression.

It may be that you have purchased or have been given this book while in the grip of a deep depression. If this is so then you may not feel very interested in poring over these pages. However, before you put the booklet down, let me make a statement which I hope will encourage you to read on – *depression can be overcome*! I can certainly understand if you react negatively to that statement, but my experiences in counselling (now extending over 30 years) have shown me conclusively that depression *can* be cured. I hope that you will read on and give me the opportunity to reinforce that statement with some facts concerning certain well-tried and proven principles which have helped thousands break free from this deeply disturbing problem.

1

What is depression?

Depression is a mood swing, in which a person is cast into varying degrees of sadness, melancholy and hopelessness. The first clinical description of depression was made by *Hippocrates* in the 2nd century AD. It was known then as 'melancholia' and a person suffering from this condition was said to be 'sad, dismayed, sleepless, becoming thin by agitation and loss of refreshing sleep . . . at a more advanced state, they complain of a thousand futilities and a desire for death'. The oldest book known, the Book of Job, describes depression in this way:

> And so to me also have been allotted months of frustration, these long and weary nights. When I go to bed I think, 'Oh, that it were morning,' and then I toss till dawn. My skin is filled with worms and blackness. My flesh breaks open, full of pus. My life flies by – day after hopeless day. My life is but a breath, and nothing good is left.
>
> (Job 7:3–7, TLB)

Depression in modern terms can best be described as a feeling of utter hopelessness, despondency, self-disgust, loss of perspective, overall gloom, sadness, apathy, dejection and despair.

2

Who gets depressed?

At some point or period in life, nearly everyone gets depressed. It is no respecter of persons, for it moves amongst all classes; the rich and the poor, the privileged and the under-privileged, the educated and the uneducated. Studies show that it occurs more in women than in men, and a higher incidence is seen in the upper end of socio-economic groups. Christians, too, can be caught in its grip. In fact, when a Christian succumbs to depression, he often suffers more painful, negative feelings than a non-Christian, due to guilt. He feels guilty that as a Christian, who is supposed to reflect the happiness and joy of the Christian faith, he is downcast by depression, and this serves only to reinforce the problem. The problem deepens when he meets with insensitive Christians who say such things as, 'Snap out of it,' or 'You shouldn't feel that way.' It is true that Jesus said, 'These things have I spoken to you . . . that your joy might be full' (John 15:11), but when a believer is caught in feelings of deep depression, and is unable to express that joy, believe me, there is not one more understanding and more caring than Jesus Christ. He doesn't stand over you in judgment, but comes alongside you in an attitude of love and care to help you recover your spiritual equilibrium and poise. So, remember, *depression is not a sin*. In some cases, it may be triggered off by sin (such as the harbouring of sinful thoughts and attitudes) but depression in and of itself is not sin. It is a symptom or signal of an inner disturbance that needs attention. There are good reasons why people stagger beneath the crushing weight of depression. All human behaviour has a cause. What, then, are the causes of depression? According to Paul in 1 Thessalonians 5:23, there are three distinct and separate parts to our personality – 'spirit, soul and body'. Depression can be caused by a disorder in any of these areas, or from a combination of any two or all three. Let's look at each of these areas in turn.

3

The physiological causes of depression

Sometimes a physical basis, or a physical factor, can be the root cause of depression. Alan, a 32 year-old engineer, who came to me for counselling over what he described as 'crippling depression', discovered this. During the first session of counselling with Alan, I suggested that before we went any further in arranging counselling sessions, he ought to see his doctor and got a thorough medical check-up. He did so and reported back to me later that the doctor had diagnosed his depression as 'endogenous'. The word 'endogenous', pronounced en-dodj-i-nus, means 'internally generated'. Endogenous depression results when the brain and nervous system (part of the internal person) become disorganised in some way, and no longer function in the way they should. Within a few days of taking the medication, given to him by his doctor, Alan's depression cleared up. There was little or no counselling needed, and this incident with Alan taught me the importance of encouraging counsellees with depressive symptoms to have a medical examination prior to counselling. Had I not done this with Alan, I might have counselled him for weeks without any positive results.

One doctor told me that in his own medical practice, the most common type of depression he came across was one that occurred as a result of the menopause. In women, it appears at about the ages of 45 to 55; in men, at about 60 and 65. When a man or woman passes through the menopause, the physiological events that go with it produce chemical changes in the body which can, in turn, produce feelings of depression. This doesn't happen to everyone, and the question is often asked: Why does it happen to some and not to others?

Some doctors think that pre-existing factors, such as a rigid type of personality, might have something to do with it. For example, a perfectionist type of person (one who finds it difficult to cope with failure or imperfection) will crack rather than bend when too much stress appears. The alteration in hormones brought about by the menopause, produces a degree of stress which the personality cannot cope with – hence instability.

Another kind of depression in which physiological factors play a great part is what doctors call *Post-Partum Depression*. This takes place in a woman- just after she has given birth to a child. Apparently, a mother is sensitive to the changes in body chemistry and glandular metabolism brought on by the pregnancy and birth, and this represents a stress that exceeds the particular person's level of tolerance in the nervous system. Here again, the question can be asked: Why does it happen to some and not to others? The same applies – preconditioning factors, such as personality type, childhood conditioning, the person's mental and emotional resources, have something to do with it. It is evident that because we are not just physical beings (and contain mental and emotional faculties) our inner attitudes greatly affect our physiology. That is why it is difficult to pin down a problem to physical factors alone. In many cases of Post-Partum depression, proper medical treatment re-establishes the chemical balance, and the person's inner resources then take over in an efficient coping capacity.

Endogenous depression may result also from generalised body infections. When an infection invades the body, through a virus, for example, it can produce toxidity (poisons) in the brain and in the nervous system, and the person can suffer a depression which, if untreated, may last for several weeks. I recently saw this in a friend of mine, an energetic minister of the Gospel who normally went about his duties with a good deal of cheerfulness and enthusiasm. After convalescing from a serious viral illness, he became deeply despondent and melancholic. He was so alarmed by his condition that he telephoned me for advice. I recommended that he see his doctor at once. Later I learned that a two-week course of antidepressants nursed him through his problem, after which he became his usual cheerful self once again.

Another bodily disturbance which may play a major role in some cases of depression is disturbance of the endocrine glands and, more specifically, a thyroid disorder. The thyroid gland in the human body secretes a hormone called thyroxine and this hormone plays a significant role in regulation of the metabolism of the body. Under-secretion of thyroxine (technically called hypothyroidism) can lead to a slowing down of the body's metabolism, producing sluggishness, memory defects, obesity, fatigue, listlessness and depression. A lady once consulted me over what she described as 'spiritual apathy and lukewarmness'. She told me that she had no desire to read her Bible, to pray, attend church or take any interest in spiritual affairs. I spent an hour with her, but I was unable to help her very much so I suggested there might be a physiological cause for her problem. After much persuasion, she saw her doctor who found that she had a serious thyroid condition. Following treatment, she felt a good deal better and her spiritual desires soon returned. Her problem was not spiritual or even emotional. It was rooted in a malfunctioning thyroid.

Such a simple thing as not eating properly or not getting proper sleep can cause depression. The person who does not eat regular well-balanced meals or get sufficient sleep may find himself becoming depressed because he is cheating his body of the food and rest it needs in order to maintain a proper level of functioning. The cure is simple and obvious: eat right and get enough sleep. I think I have said enough to show that whenever anyone is faced with the problem of depression, careful evaluation of the physical factors is of the utmost importance. Even though, as in some cases, physical factors are not the sole cause, they can break down one's ability to tolerate stress and, therefore, compound an emotional difficulty which has arisen from another source.

4

The psychological causes of depression

Depression (as we have seen) can arise from physiological disturbances and malfunctioning, but it can arise too from problems which occur in the realm of the soul – the *psychological* part of our being. One doctors says, 'The roots of depression run deep. A person who becomes depressed for the first time at the age of 40, in all likelihood, had some contributing roots to his depression planted in the early years of his development.' Studies have shown that many of our adult behaviour patterns and attitudes are firmly entrenched by our sixth birthday. In those crucial first six years of life, we picked up our parents' attitudes and behaviour patterns (especially the parent of the same sex) and we learned to relate to life by following their example. If they repressed their anger, we too have a tendency to repress our anger. If they used illness to gain sympathy, then we tend to do the same. Time and time again, when counselling people with psychological depression, I have been able to trace the roots of it way back into their childhood. It appears that if our parents failed to love us in the way they should, or teach us, by word *and* example to relate properly to life, we carry within us the soil out of which the tree of depression can grow. One of the earliest needs of a child is to receive unconditional love and affection. Many parents, although they have a great love for their children, fail to express in a demonstrative way the love they feel in their hearts. They seldom hug, compliment, encourage, touch or show any spontaneous kind of affection, and this is subconsciously interpreted by the child as rejection or lack of concern. John Powell, a priest with the *Society of Jesus* says that in the early days of one's life, a child is like the bud of a flower or plant – *closed*. Only when the bud of the flower receives warmth from the sun and nourishment from the mothering soil, will it open and expose its latent beauty. So, too, he claims, human beings at the beginning of life need the warmth and nourishment of unconditional love if they are to open up and expose their inner beauty. If the bud of a flower is affected by hostile forces, such as severe frost or heavy winds, it will not open. 'So, too,' says John Powell, 'a human person who is without the warm encouragement of love, and who must endure the chilling absence of praise and affection, will remain closed in on himself. The dynamics of his personality will be jammed.'

Such a child, when he develops into an adult, will tend to relate to life on the basis of his early feelings – the feelings of rejection and disinterest. Feeling unloved, he comes to view himself in this way at all times, and this feeling, if allowed to continue unchecked and uncorrected, can precipitate a person into psychological depression.

Out of the soil of parental deprivation (lack of love, incorrect training, etc.) several roots develop which can, in later life, produce the problem we know as depression. One of these is *a lack of self-worth*. Almost every person I have ever counselled with psychological depression had a problem with their self-image. The problem is know in psychological circles as *self-rejection*. Each one of us has an idea of our personal worth, and the way we evaluate ourselves is called our *self-image*. Self-image is the 'map' we use to check on to evaluate our worth to ourselves, to God and to others. It is the mental picture of our self-identity, or the way we feel about ourselves deep down. We either feel good about ourselves, or we may dislike, or even hate, ourselves. Where did this self-image come from and how did it develop? The image we have of ourselves is obtained by noting the way that other people, such as parents, siblings, teachers, evaluate our appearance and our abilities. If, for example, we were continually told when we were children that we were stupid, ignorant, ugly, then this becomes the basis for the way we look at ourselves. Unless we can correct these attitudes and feelings, a difficult task, indeed, for a young child, we enter into adult life with no clear sense of our identity and worth. Nearly everything we do is influenced by the fact that we are not as adequate or important as others, and these dynamics of self-rejection can lead, in due course, to psychological depression.

Another root that grows in the soil of parental deprivation is that of *anger*. Do you ever remember, as a child, saying to your father, 'Daddy, I'm feeling angry with you right now; can we talk about it?' The truth is that most probably you were never taught how to express your anger, and thus you come to fear it, rather than share it. A child soon realises that getting angry just doesn't pay because it results in rejection or punishment, so he learns to deceive himself into thinking that he wasn't really angry at all, or he represses his anger and then displaces it by kicking the dog or fighting with his brothers or sisters.

Many people believe that anger plays a major part in the development of depression. They describe it as 'inverted anger' – anger turned inwards on oneself. I once put this idea in these terms to a man I counselled who was suffering from depression: 'How would you respond to the idea that you are angry with yourself?' He at once rejected the idea and said, 'Everyone will tell you I am the most placid person you could ever hope to meet.' But as we talked and went deeper into his life, he began to see, and later admitted, that repressed deep inside him was, as he described, a 'volcano of anger waiting to erupt'. Don't be surprised if you find yourself rejecting the idea that you can be inwardly angry. Think it through with me a little more.

If during our growing up years, we sense that we are not being given the love and attention we need then we experience a number of negative emotions – despair, insecurity, rejection *and* anger. But when anger arises, we face a problem. If we become angry with our parents, we run the risk of alienating ourselves from the very source we need to survive. So we repress the anger, and shut it up in the subconscious. Let me share with you how anger, lying in the personality and then turned inwards, worked to produce depression in one of my counsellees.

21

Mark, a 35 year-old accountant, became depressed when he was passed over for a promotion he thought he deserved. In a counselling session, I asked him if he felt angry about the situation. 'Me? angry?' he said, 'I can't ever remember being angry over anything.' Actually Mark was *very* angry, but he had learned to repress his anger and not admit it to himself. He was holding an unconscious grudge against his superiors, and when at last he recognised his anger, and admitted it, his depression lifted as if by magic.

Another root problem that can contribute to the development of depression is *false guilt*. True guilt is valuable but false guilt is not. God uses true guilt to influence us to change our mind about what we are doing. That's what repentance is all about. When we do what is right instead of what is wrong, we are in fellowship with God and we tend to feel good about ourselves. Doing what is wrong lowers our feeling of self-worth; doing what is right greatly improves our feeling of self-worth. Sometimes people feel guilty because they are guilty – this is real guilt. The components of psychological depression, however, are not real guilt but false guilt. What, then, is false guilt? False guilt usually results from faulty relationships in the developmental years. Too rigid a parent with excessively high standards and rigid expectations, can develop in a child a conscience that is overly strict, so much so that the child feels guilty when he falls short of those standards. There is nothing wrong with high standards, of course, providing the parents make it clear that if the child fails to live up to them, he is still an accepted member of the family. Parents who excessively blame their children, or condemn them without a fair hearing, create feelings of false guilt. Unforgiving parents who punish excessively also create guilt. Adequate and proper punishment given in love removes guilt. Some parents are never satisfied and no matter how well the child performs in school or at sports, the parents make him feel he ought to have done better. The child then sees himself as a constant failure, and experiences deep feelings of false guilt. Such a child, when he becomes an adult, carries these inner feelings of false guilt into his work, his marriage, indeed, *all* his relationships, and it can, in some cases, work itself out in the form of depression.

Feelings of self-depreciation and guilt, which have been created by misguided parents, must be dealt with by examining the experiences which led to the formation of these attitudes. False guilt is feeling guilty about something that God and His Word in no way condemn. As a person begins to see that he is suffering from a guilt which is not the result of the conviction of the Holy Spirit, he can gain a new relief and a new freedom.

Yet another root problem that can contribute to depression is *excessive dependency*. If we have never been taught how to stand on our own two feet, then we will either seek something to lean on for external support or props to hold ourselves up. This is why dependency relationships characterise the lives of those who are depressed. Beryl, a 30 year-old nurse, married with two children, told me that she had struggled for over ten years with the problem of depression. In a counselling session, she told me that she had been raised by a very dominant mother who would never let her stand on her own two feet. Mother had made all the decisions for her – what she was to wear, where she was to go, what musical instrument she had to play, and so on. Her marriage was not happy, and as we talked about the early part of her life, she came to see that she had gone into marriage in order to trade off one dependency relationship for another. I asked Beryl to describe her husband for me and, unwittingly, she used the same words to describe her husband that she had used to describe her mother – dominant, inconsiderate, self-centred, angry, judgmental and opinionated. It became clear that Beryl had been drawn to her husband because she saw in him characteristics that could meet her deep need for dependency. However, now, after experiencing problems in her marriage, she wondered whether she had jumped from the frying pan into the fire.

Beryl had never been her own person. Her mother had prevented her from developing into an independent human being. She hated her mother, and now she had grown to hate her husband. She was trapped in a relationship that angered her. On the one hand, she longed to be independent yet on the other, she felt herself so utterly dependent. For Beryl, life was a very precarious existence. She lived in fear that she would lose the person on whom she relied – her husband – and it was this excessive dependency that precipitated her depression. In times of stress and strain, Beryl was unable to draw upon internal psychological resources simply because there was nothing there but an aching void. Eventually, as she came to see herself as God saw her – a worthwhile human being – and she accepted the Lord into her life, she became a more secure and self-possessed person, and her depression disappeared.

In some cultures, more females struggle with depression than males, at about a ratio of three to one. The reason for this lies right here with the matter of dependency. Females, in some societies, have been taught to be dependent and passive. Also, some females have lacked a basis on which to establish their identity. Many churches, for example, have presented the principle of submission, as expressed by Paul in Ephesians 5:22, in such a way that women have regarded their role as one of servility rather than submissiveness. No woman can be truly submissive until she first has a clear sense of her identity, and becomes assertive in the best sense of the word.

Another root cause of depression is *faulty thinking*. In fact, the trend in modern-day psychiatry is to view faulty thinking as being a prime cause of many of our emotional problems. The Bible suggests that the thoughts we think have a great deal to do with the way we act and feel (Proverbs 23:7). Dr Albert Ellis, an American psychologist, has a simple model for explaining the relationship between thinking and feeling. It is called the A-B-C Theory of Behaviour. A equals the event or problem one faces. B equals the way we perceive that event – our evaluation of it. C is the consequent emotion that results from how we perceive the event.

A = the event
B = our evaluation of the event
C = the consequent emotion

According to Ellis, we cannot move from A to C without going through B. In other words, no event or problem can arouse within us a negative emotion. What produces the emotion is our evaluation of the event – the way we perceive it. Let's take a specific example to clarify the issue still further. Have you ever felt angry when someone criticised you unjustly? Well, according to Ellis' theory (and it is one that I fully support) there is no way that someone's criticism of you can make you angry, for A does not control C. What made you angry was the way you interpreted that event to yourself. You probably said to yourself, 'It hurts to be criticised. I don't like the feeling of worthlessness it creates inside me. I will retaliate, therefore, by becoming angry at the person who criticised me.' Of course, these sentences are not conscious, but deep down inside you something like this would be going on. It is not what is said *but what we think about what is said* that produces the negative emotion.

The pattern for faulty thinking begins, as do the other root problems we discussed, in early childhood. A child who gets the notion that he is incapable or inferior, either as a result of failure or being called incapable by others, tends to respond to all the experiences of life according to this belief. And every new negative judgment tends to reinforce the previous ones so that a vicious cycle is set in motion.

Negative or faulty thinking can soon plunge a person into depression. The person with a negative view of himself, of the world and of life in general, interprets all experiences as detracting from rather than adding to his identity. Even neutral experiences are seen in a negative light. An innocent remark by a friend is interpreted as rejection. An innocuous statement is regarded as hostile. His thinking pattern is clouded by reading into the remarks of others things which fit his previously drawn negative conclusions. He is so predisposed to negative thinking that he automatically forms negative conclusions about most of life's situations.

In one counselling session, where I counselled a man with severe depression, I set up an arrangement whereby he would check on himself to discover how many times a day he found himself thinking negatively. This was the arrangement – I got him to wear on his wrist a rubber band and gave him instructions that every time he found himself thinking a negative thought, he must give himself a sharp twang with the rubber band. The next time I saw him (a week later) his wrist was red and sore. 'I could never have believed,' he said, 'how many times a day a negative thought arises in my mind unless I saw it so dramatically demonstrated in this manner.' In his case, the gradual challenging and changing of negative thought patterns was responsible, more than any one thing, for bringing him up from the pit of depression.

Some readers, maybe you, will experience twinges of despair after reading the above paragraph. Yet there is nothing disturbing about it. If anything, the paragraph should bring hope. Then what caused you to feel a twinge of despair? It was your *thought*: 'This may work for other people, but I doubt it would work for me.' Or, 'It sounds too much like hard work. Surely there are easier ways of overcoming my problem than this?' The thought may even have been: 'I don't care if thousands of other people get better – I'm convinced, beyond any shadow of doubt, that my problems are hopeless.' This delusion reflects the kind of mental processing that is at the very core of your problem.

Several years ago, a doctor conducted a pilot study, comparing cognitive therapy (the process of challenging and changing negative thought patterns) with one of the most widely used antidepressant drugs on the market, Tofranil. Over 40 severely depressed patients were randomly assigned to two groups. One group received cognitive therapy and no drugs. The other group received Tofranil and no cognitive therapy. Both groups of patients were treated for a twelve-week period. The outcome of this study was that cognitive therapy showed itself to be substantially superior to antidepressant drugs in all respects. (These findings are reported in *Feeling Good: the New Mood Therapy* by David D. Burns, MD; page 14, Signet Books, USA.)

5

The spiritual causes of depression

We have seen how depression can arise from physical and psychological causes so we move now to a consideration of the third dimension of man's being – the spirit. God created each one of us so that we could relate to Him and unless we have a vital relationship with God, through His Son, Jesus Christ, we can never experience true happiness or contentment. Several years ago, I heard of a woman who visited a Harley Street psychiatrist, and asked him to treat her for her depression. The psychiatrist set up several expensive sessions of therapy, at the end of which, she was no better. The psychiatrist used a combination of drugs and psychotherapy, but it was all to no avail. One Sunday evening, however, she attended a central London church where she heard a minister explain the way of salvation. The minister said (amongst other things) that because each one of us is separated from God by our sin, we carry inside us a deep problem of guilt. This guilt can only be dissolved in our hearts when we accept the benefits of Christ's atonement on the Cross. At the end of the service, the woman went to the minister and asked him to pray with her because she wanted to receive Jesus Christ into her life as her Lord and Saviour. When she did this, she found, almost immediately, that the depression which had been with her for several years completely disappeared. She became a new woman – overnight. Later, when the woman was introduced to me at the end of a service where I had been preaching, I questioned her very closely about her conversion. 'How do you account for the fact,' I asked, 'that although no one could cure your depression, it left you suddenly the night you were converted?' With a smile, she said, 'My problem was not so much psychological guilt but *real* guilt. My psychiatrist, I think, could have dealt with my psychological guilt, but God, and only God, could deal with my real guilt.'

Earlier we talked about false guilt – the psychological problem some people face which is due to improper parenting. We must now face the fact that there is a real form of guilt – guilt which descends upon the human spirit whenever one or more of God's principles have been violated. Although every person who has not committed himself to Jesus Christ is a sinner in God's sight (Romans 3:23) not everyone feels that guilt subjectively. This is because the human heart is adept at producing defence mechanisms, such as rationalisation, projection, displacement and so on, devices which minimise the pain of spiritual guilt. One of the ministries of the Holy Spirit is to make a person *feel* guilty before God. 'When he is come,' said Jesus, speaking of the coming of the Holy Spirit, 'He will reprove the world of sin, and of righteousness, and of judgment . . .' (John 16:8). Multitudes of Christians can tell how, prior to their conversion, they found themselves in the throes of deep inner conflict as they struggled against the gentle pleadings of the Holy Spirit. This conflict, if not resolved by acceptance of God's gift of salvation and the forgiveness of sins, can lead to a spiritual form of depression. What release, however, as one repents of sin, receives forgiveness and enters into God's glorious salvation!

Spiritual depression can also be experienced by Christians who sin and fail to turn to Christ for forgiveness. In fact, true guilt, and the resulting depression, should be the normal experience of Christians who resist confessing any known sin. Many godly people have suffered from depression because of sin and true guilt. King David said, 'When I kept silent about my sin, my bones wasted away through my groaning all day long. For day and night your hand was heavy upon me, my strength was sapped as in the heat of summer' (Psalm 32:3, NIV). In the first epistle of John, chapter 3, the apostle says, 'Dear children, do not let anyone lead you astray. He who does what is right is righteous, just as he is righteous. He who does what is sinful is of the devil, because the devil has been sinning from the beginning . . . No one who is born of God will continue to sin, because God's seed remains in him; he cannot sin, because he has been born of God' (vs. 7–9, NIV). 'No one who lives in him keeps on sinning' (v. 6, NIV). These verses indicate that anyone who habitually chooses and wilfully practises a known sin is not a Christian. Of course, Christians sin daily, and continually need to claim God's promise to forgive them their sins. A true Christian, however, will not be able to wilfully continue in a known sin for a very long time without experiencing guilt and depression. Let us be quite clear about this issue for it is often misinterpreted. The Bible is not saying that a true Christian never sins. It is saying that a true Christian cannot *practise* sin. Christ's life within him will not permit him to live a life of practising sin.

Another precipitating cause of spiritual depression in Christians is a wrong perspective on life. In a world such as we live in, it is easy for Christians to get their eyes focused on wrong perspectives. In Psalm 73:1–3, Asaph records the depression he felt when he developed a wrong perspective:

Surely God is good to Israel, to those who are pure in heart. But as for me, my feet had almost slipped; I had nearly lost my foothold. For I envied the arrogant when I saw the prosperity of the wicked. (NIV)

In verses 16 and 17, it seems he finally got his perspective right and his depression lifted.

When I tried to understand all this, it was oppressive to me till I entered the sanctuary of God; then I understood their final destiny. (NIV)

A wrong perspective on life is to see things from our point of view rather than from God's point of view. One of my favourite verses of Scripture is Colossians 1:9 which in the J. B. Phillips paraphrase reads: 'Pray that you will see things as it were from God's point of view.' Time and time again, I have watched spiritual depression lift in people who learn to get their priorities straight, and learn to look at life from God's point of view.

Another major source of spiritual depression in

Christians results from a failure to establish proper priorities. Our first priority as Christians is getting to know God more intimately (see Philippians 3:10). Next we should focus on meeting the needs of our family (see 1 Timothy 5:8). This includes our work or profession, for it is through this that we obtain the finances to meet their needs. Then with the time we have left over, we should concentrate on ministering to others along the line of particular gifts which God has given us. Some Christians, because of unconscious psychological drives within them and a strong need for approval, neglect their family in order to 'serve the Lord'. Many ministers, missionaries and full-time Christian workers fall into this category. They put their ministry before their family and then wonder why the Lord allows them to burn themselves out or finish up in deep depression.

Finally another precipitating factor of spiritual depression is a direct attack by Satan. The apostle Peter tells us that 'Your enemy the devil prowls around like a roaring lion looking for someone to devour' (1 Peter 5:8, NIV). Early in my ministry (1952–53) I remember going through a period of depression which greatly alarmed me. I submitted to a thorough medical examination and passed A1. I then examined my thoughts and attitudes to see whether there was something going on in my personality that could be contributing to the problem. I found nothing. One day, while in prayer, the thought came to me that this was perhaps an attack of Satan. The devil likes nothing better than to render Christians ineffective in any way he can; and one way is through depression. The more I prayed about the matter, the more convinced I became that Satan was trying to harass me and my ministry through this means. I did something that day in prayer that I have never done before and have never done since. I laid my own hands on my head and said, 'Satan, I rebuke you in the Name of Jesus. Get out of my personality right now. Be gone and never return.' I found release within minutes, and, praise God, I have never experienced that particular kind of attack since that day, now close on 30 years ago. Don't, however, jump to the wrong conclusion and think that all depression is a direct attack of Satan. Consider and evaluate the situation carefully through a process of elimination. Look into the physical area first. If there is nothing wrong there, check the psychological. If nothing shows up there, check the spiritual area very carefully. If you feel that your spiritual life is in order, ask God to show you if the problem is the direct result of Satan's efforts to render you ineffective. If as you wait before the Lord, you are assured of this, then do what the Scripture says: 'Resist the devil, and he will flee from you' (James 4:7).

6

The common denominator

In all types of depression a common denominator can be found – *loss*. Did you notice how much the *idea* of loss was involved in the causes of depression we examined in the last few pages? In the physiological area, it was loss of physical efficiency. In the psychological area, it was loss of personal identity. In the spiritial area, it was loss of contact with God. I believe it true to say that in many, if not most depressions, there is a loss of some kind involved. And, in some cases, it is not so much actual loss but imagined loss. Several years ago, a lady used to ring me up every few days to tell me that she was depressed because God was no longer interested in her. I knew her to be a Christian, and attempted to reassure her that, despite her feelings, God was committed to staying with her in all her difficulties because He had promised, 'I will never leave you, nor forsake you.' My advice didn't seem to help very much, so I invited her to come for counselling. In the sessions, she came to see that her depression resulted not from a loss of God's interest but from her *fear* of the loss. When we dealt with her fear, which was rooted deep in her early childhood experiences, she was a transformed person.

The Old Testament account of God's servant Job portrays in vivid detail the role that loss (whether real or imagined) plays in triggering off depression.

Job lost almost everything it's possible to lose. He lost his wealth as well as his means of livelihood. He lost his servants. He even lost his children. Finally, he lost his health. As a result, Job plunged into the depths of depression. Listen to what he says:

May the day of my birth perish, and the night it was said, 'A boy is born!' That day – may it turn to darkness; may God above not care about it; may no light shine upon it. Why did I not perish at birth, and die as I came from the womb? . . . For now I would be lying down in peace . . . (Job 3:3, 4, 11 and 13, NIV).

The most moving thing about the story of Job is the fact that, despite his depression, he still clung to his faith in God. Someone once said, 'Never let go in the dark what you received in the light.' Job did that. Although physically broken and deeply dispirited, he affirmed that God was still in control of his life, and that a wise and loving purpose was at work in his circumstances. Listen to what he says in Job 13:15, 'Though he slay me, yet will I trust in him.' And again in Job 19:25, he affirms: 'I know that my Redeemer lives, and that in the end he will stand upon the earth' (NIV). What amazing faith!

7

Seven steps to overcoming depression

It is time now to consider what practical steps can be take to overcome the feelings of depression. These seven steps I am about to give you have been used time and time again by hundreds of people suffering from the malady, and I hope you gain the same positive results from them as have others.

Firstly, if your depression is deep and longstanding, get a complete medical check-up. If you are suffering from an underactive thyroid, hypoglycemia, or some other significant physical condition, then counselling will be of limited value. Notice that I did not say it would be of no value, but *limited* value. If the basic problem is a physical one, then it is only when that is dealt with that real progress can be made in the psychological and spiritual areas of your life.

The question is often asked me by counsellees: If, after I have had a medical check-up, no significant physical cause is discovered, should I continue to use antidepressants? There are some Christians who would say no. They regard it as deeply unspiritual to rely on medication since (they say) we should rely entirely on the Lord. I am not of that opinion. Dr Q. Quentin Hyder, a psychiatrist and a Christian, says, 'As a Christian physician, I use two weapons to help my patients conquer depression. Physically, for the body, I prescribe a brief course of antidepressants. They are to be taken only for a short time, and they work by reducing the mood-lowering effect of certain temporary chemical imbalances in the blood. They make the patient feel better, but are only an expedient in mood elevation to tide him over the difficult period until the second weapon – Christian counselling – can produce a more permanent cure.'

It is only a few decades ago that a large number of Christians thought it a sin to wear glasses. They called them the 'devil's eyes'. They reasoned that if God wanted you to be able to see He would have given you good vision. One doctor reports, 'Even after the discovery of penicillin, many Christians died of pneumonia because they wanted to trust God alone and not medication.' I believe it right to use judiciously the benefits of modern science. I say judiciously because there are some so-called cures for depression which I regard as extremely suspect. I would never encourage a person to submit to insulin coma therapy, for example, or electroconvulsive therapy (ECT) because I believe that in these approaches there is a potential risk to the patient and, in many, they bring only temporary relief. I do not believe in the use of addictive medication either. If you are in doubt about the medication your doctor gives you, have a frank talk with him or her, and express your fears or concerns. Most doctors (if not all) will be glad to explain their reasons for the medication they prescribe for you.

If, after having a medical check-up, no significant physical factor is found to be the cause, then focus your attention on the following considerations. Indeed, even though a physical cause may be found, you will still benefit greatly from the suggestions I am now going to make.

Secondly, *give up all grudges and forgive everyone who has hurt you or offended you*. Earlier we saw that many problems arise in our lives because of deprivation in our childhood. This deprivation, more often than not, brings about resentment and bitterness in our hearts. We feel inwardly angry that our basic needs were not met and this can cause us to become bearers of grudges. We may bear a grudge against our parents (albeit unconsciously), against ourselves (self-deprivation) or against God for allowing things to be the way they were. 'Accumulated grudges,' says a medical doctor, 'contribute to the biochemical changes that set up a depression.' You can't afford to live with a grudge in your heart so, right now, forgive everyone who has ever hurt you or sinned against you. I have never known a person suffering from non-organic depression (i.e. depression not caused by a physiological problem) who did not carry a grudge of some sort in their heart. Evelyn, a fine young schoolteacher, who came to me for counselling over her depression, greatly resisted the idea when I put it to her that one of the components of her depression might be a grudge. 'I carry a grudge against no one,' was her reply. 'And what is more,' she went on, 'if you think I might be nursing an unconscious grudge against my parents, then I can assure you that is not so.' Despite Evelyn's protestations, I felt it right to invite her to co-operate with me in the process which counsellors describe as 'the healing of the memories'. I don't always practise this in counselling, except on rare occasions, but this time I felt a gentle tug from the Holy Spirit, leading me in this direction. The healing of the memories is a simple counselling procedure whereby a person is taken back over their past so that through prayer and the guidance and help of the Holy Spirit, painful memories which have been repressed can be brought up into consciousness and healed. Evelyn was hesitant at first but eventually we began to work back over her past life until we came to a time when she was about seven years old, and the Holy Spirit brought to her mind a memory of an event (which she claimed she had completely forgotten) when her parents were engaged in a violent quarrel. As the scene flashed before her, she described to me in vivid detail how her father took a carving knife from the kitchen table and held it to her mother's throat, threatening to take her life. Evelyn began to sob violently, and said through clenched teeth, 'How I hate my father for that. I thought I had no animosity in my heart but now I see I have never forgiven him for that action against my mother.' The event had been forgotten by the conscious mind, but the unconscious mind never forgets anything. I encouraged her to hold the image of her father in her mind and say, 'Daddy, although I had never really forgiven you for that action I do so now – in Jesus' Name.' There were several other smaller grudges in Evelyn's life which came out in that session and when these were all dealt with Evelyn appeared to be a new woman. She left the counselling room as if she was walking on air.

Not all depressed people need the ministry of the healing of the memories. I rarely proceed in this direction unless clearly drawn by the Holy Spirit, and *never* until I have eliminated most of the other approaches.

A grudge can be carried, not only against others, but against oneself. Sometimes the most difficult person to forgive is *yourself* if your are what psychologists call a 'perfectionist type' – someone who strives endlessly to reach up to extremely high standards in everything they do, then when they fall below the standards, even for genuine and good reasons, they find it difficult to forgive themselves. I myself fall into the category of a perfectionist, but over the years I have learned, thankfully, to cope with the problems my type of personality presents. When I first began preaching, if I preached a sermon I considered to be beneath my usual standard, I would become severely depressed. I would say to myself, 'What a mess you made of that! If only you hadn't forgotten that important point. Why did you miss out the illustration you had so carefully prepared? You went on far too long,' and so on. One day God said to me, 'Selwyn, don't you realise I am blessing you despite your imperfections? Rest in me. All I ask is for your sincerity, and given that, I can work through all your imperfections.' Now, whenever I fall beneath my own high standards, I simply rest in God, and trust Him to bring to pass His purposes. I have learned how to come to terms with the fact that even though I could do better *his is the way it is*. As I accept that fact and forgive myself for not attaining the standards I hold in my mind, I

41

am free from pressure and am more able to focus on the next task to hand. There is nothing wrong with high standards, providing we recognise that at times, and for good reasons, we may not be able to reach up to them. At such times we must accept ourselves as we are and learn to trust God to work through our imperfections to glorify His Name.

It is possible to carry a grudge, not only against others or against yourself, but against God. A minister's wife, in a seminar where I was sharing some of the concepts I am sharing with you now, said to me, 'I never realised before that I was carrying a grudge against God for not healing me. It came home so clearly to me today. I have asked the Lord to forgive me and I am assured He has. Now I feel a completely different woman.' Many Christians carry an unconscious grudge against God over a variety of issues. We may resent the fact He didn't answer our prayers in the way we thought He should, or that His answer came too late. We may even be unconsciously bitter that God allowed a loved one to be taken from us, or that He permitted hard and difficult circumstances to come our way when we were least able to cope. We must examine our hearts and run a check on our spiritual lives to see whether we are inwardly resentful against God. A good way to test yourself is to read Romans 8:28-29, and ask yourself: 'Can I fully accept, without equivocation, that a sovereign God is so committed to me in love that He will never allow anything to happen to me unless it accords with His wise and loving purpose for me?' This means that everything He has allowed He has done so because

He foresaw it would work for your benefit and for His eternal glory. If you can accept that, not merely in your head, but with your heart, and give yourself to it in glad and total abandonment, then you will respond to everything that comes your way, not with a grudge but with gratitude. One thing is sure, unless we learn to give up all our grudges, grudges against others, against ourselves or against God, we will never know lasting victory over depression.

Thirdly, *begin work on restructuring your thought patterns*. We have already seen in our discussion of the *ABC Theory of Behaviour* that our thoughts greatly affect our emotions. We feel and act the way we do largely because of the thoughts that go through our minds, consciously and subconsciously. After dealing with hundreds of depressed people over the years, I have noticed one thing in particular – depressed people have thoughts that are shot through with negative attitudes and ideas. And when these negative attitudes and ideas are challenged and changed into positive ones, depression begins to lift. Most of these negative thoughts are, of course, *automatic*. The mind has entertained them for so long they become an accepted part of the personality.

David D. Burns, MD, in his book *Feeling Good: The New Mood Therapy*, says that there are ten major thought distortions that arise in a depressed person's thoughts. He list them as follows:

1. *All or nothing thinking*. You see things in black and white categories. If your performance falls short of perfect, you see yourself as a total failure.
2. *Overgeneralisation*. You see a single negative

event as a never-ending pattern of defeat.

3. *Mental filter*. You pick out a single negative detail and dwell on it exclusively so that your vision of all reality becomes darkened like the drop of ink that discolours the entire glass of water.

4. *Disqualifying the positive*. You reject positive experiences by insisting they 'don't count' for some reason or other. In this way, you can maintain a negative belief that is contradicted by your everyday experiences.

5. *Jumping to conclusions*. You make a negative interpretation even though there are no definite facts that convincingly support the conclusion.

6. *Magnification or minimisation*. You exaggerate the importance of things (such as your own failure or someone else's achievements), or you inappropriately shrink things until they appear tiny (your own desirable qualities or the other person's imperfections). This is also called the 'binocular trick'.

7. *Emotional reasoning*. You assume that your negative emotions necessarily reflect the way things really are – 'I feel it; therefore it must be true.'

8. *'Should' statements*. You try to motivate yourself with should's and shouldn'ts, as if you have to be whipped and punished before you could be expected to do anything. 'Must's' and 'ought's' are also offenders. The emotional consequence is guilt.

9. *Labelling and mis-labelling*. An extreme form of overgeneralisation. Instead of describing your error, you attach a negative label to yourself – 'I'm a *loser*.' When someone else's behaviour rubs you up the wrong way, you attach a negative label to him –

'He's a louse.' Mis-labelling involves describing an event with language that is highly coloured and emotionally loaded.

10. *Personalisation*. You see yourself as the cause of some negative, external event which, in fact, you are not primarily responsible for.

The first step in restructuring your thought patterns is to identify the thoughts that go on in your head. If you are a housewife and your husband complains that the meal you cooked was faulty, what thought crosses your mind? It may be so fast, you can miss it, but, believe me, it is there. Isn't it something like this: 'I can't do anything right. I'm a total failure. I can't stand this. I work like a slave and this is the thanks I get. The brute.' These thoughts soon trigger off negative emotions because, as we are seeing, our emotions follow our thoughts just like baby ducks follow their mother. Ask yourself which of your distortions include one or more of the following:

a. All or nothing thinking
b. Overgeneralisation
c. Magnification
d. Labelling

Actually the distortion I described above includes all of them. When you tell yourself, 'I can't do anything right,' you are *overgeneralising*. Of course, you can do some things, probably many things right. When you say, 'I'm a total failure,' you are engaging in '*all or nothing thinking*'. So stop it at once. The meal may not have been up to your usual standard but it doesn't make your life a total failure. When you say, 'I can't stand this,' you are *magnifying* the pain you are feeling. You are blowing it up out of all proportion. You are standing it, and if you are, you can. Finally, when you say to yourself, 'I work like a slave and this is the thanks I get. The brute,' you are *labelling* both yourself and your husband. He's not a brute. He's just being insensitive. And you are not a slave. You are just letting your husband's irritability ruin your evening.

Wear an elastic band around your wrist for a few days and twang it every time you catch yourself thinking a negative thought, like the man I mentioned earlier. Identify the distortion in your thinking, and see if it fits into one of the categories described by David Burns.

Next, after you have discovered what category the thought fits into (keep in mind that this will take you several days of practice), then challenge the distortion, and pinpoint exactly why it is inaccurate or untrue. Say to yourself, 'I'm jumping to conclusions again.' Or, 'There I go – overgeneralising. It's about time I straightened out my thinking in this direction, once and for all.' Or, 'Perhaps I'm falling into the trap of emotional reasoning – because I feel this way I am believing it must be true.' Distinguish between ideas and facts. Feelings are not facts. A person's thoughts do not always represent reality, and they should be examined carefully before being accepted.

Finally, replace negative thinking by positive thoughts about yourself – thoughts that are true and in keeping with what God says about you. A Christian does not have to be dominated by old patterns of thought derived from the past. Listen to what Paul says about this: 'God has not given us the spirit of fear; but of power, and of love, and of a sound mind' (2 Timothy 1:7). Soundness means that the new mind can do what it is supposed to do – think God's thoughts after Him. Spend time with the Bible and discover what God thinks about you, and what are His purposes for your life.

When, for example, a thought like this comes, 'I'm a failure,' then counter it with Ephesians 1:6 – 'To the praise of the glory of his grace, wherein he hath made us accepted in the beloved.' Say to yourself, 'God says I am predestined to the praise of His glory and that means He is going to get rewards from my life despite all my shortcoming, *for God has never failed to finish anything He has begun!*' Perhaps you may have a thought that says, 'I've been shaped by the past and it is too late to change.' Counter it with 2 Corinthians 5:17 – 'When someone becomes a Christian he becomes a brand new person inside. He is not the same any more. A new life has begun!' (TLB). When a thought arises in your mind similar to this, 'Just when everything seemed to be coming right for me then this happens,' counter it with Romans 8:28 – 'And we know that all that happens to us is working for our good if we love God and are fitting into his plans.' (TLB). Say to yourself, 'God knows what is best for my life and He would never have allowed this to happen unless it can work for my benefit and for His glory.'

There is a Scripture verse to suit every situation that ever occurs in your life. Purchase a copy of 'Let The Living Bible Help You' by Alice Zillman Chapin (published by Fountain/Collins), which lists key passages that relate to human problems such as fear, worry, loneliness, anxiety, humiliation and so on.

So remember these three crucial steps when attempting to restructure your thoughts:

- Identify the thoughts that go on in your head. Don't let them buzz around in your brain; snare them by tracking them down. Study the ten distortions and see if it fits into one of the categories.
- Challenge the distortion and tell yourself precisely why it is untrue and inaccurate.
- Replace the wrong thinking by the positive Scripture assurances from God's Word.

Fourthly, *engage in physical exercise*. Exercise is essential for good digestion, and good elimination. It is helpful, too, for maintaining muscle tone and endurance. But more to the point perhaps, it is essential for the maintenance of good emotional balance. Not many years ago, our way of life required a good deal of physical activity from us, but not any more. We have become generally-speaking an inactive, spectator-oriented society. We are overweight and underexercised. We watch when we could participate. We complain because we are so tired and yet we have done nothing exhaustive. Nothing *physically* exhausting, that is, but, nevertheless, we *really* are tired. Modern life is lived at great speed and under great pressure, and we rarely get enough physical release from the stimulation and arousal that life in the 20th century produces. We accumulate all kinds of tensions as we move from one day to another – our muscles get tight and our blood pressure shoots up. A depressed person becomes more physically tense than other people because they are more easily aroused emotionally; their bodies tighten like a drum. When we are tense or when our minds are full of all sorts of threats and burdens and problems, we find it difficult to sleep. The next day, we are unable to mobilise sufficient energy to combat our problems, and so we go on from day to day in a state of semi-exhaustion. This sets up a vicious circle that reinforces the depression.

On many occasions I have recommended to depressed people an exercise or fitness programme, and have seen the vicious circle of exhaustion broken, even when some of the more basic problems have not yet been fully resolved. When a depressed person uses up nervous energy and tension through physical exercise, this at least allows them to get some sleep. The next day they are in a much better state physically to confront their problems with great vigour and stamina. It would be inadvisable, however, to embark upon a strenuous programme of exercise without first consulting your doctor. He may know of good reasons why physical exercise may, in your case, be counter-productive. So check with your physician first.

While on this subject of the care of the human body, let me mention another problem which needs to be brought under control – *overweight*. One doctor said, 'We dig our graves with our teeth!' We really do. One of the great sins of today, which we hear little about in Christian circles, is gluttony. About six or seven years ago, God spoke to me about this sin through a friend who drew my attention to the fact that I was a good deal overweight. What happened to me is what happens to most people – gaining weight was a gradual process. Somehow, before I realised what was happening, it had already happened. It took me several weeks of dieting and exercise to get down to my ideal weight. When I eventually got there, the results were astonishing. I found that I could get through my day with the minimum of difficulty, and my power of concentration increased tremendously. By the way, I still have a weight problem, inasmuch as I gain weight very easily. I stay on a fairly low calorie diet, however, and have a regular programme of exercise, so that I can maintain my ideal weight and be as fit as I can possibly be for the service of my Master, the Lord Jesus Christ. Paul told the Corinthians: 'What? know ye not that your body is the temple of the Holy Ghost which is in you, which ye have of God, and ye are not your own. For ye are bought with a price: therefore glorify God in your body, and in your spirit, which are God's' (1 Corinthians 6:19–20). Take a look at your body right now. Does it glorify God? Is it a fit temple for Him to dwell in? Now if this sounds challenging, don't shrink back in despair and say, 'I could never muster the will power to begin a programme of exercise or cut down on my food intake.' The truth is, you can. I think I have demonstrated in these pages that I am extremely sympathetic to the condition of a depressed person, but there are times when it is right to speak straight and to the point. This is one of them. Stop feeling sorry for yourself and throw your will into line with the Lord Jesus Christ. He not only asks you to reach up to what might seem unbelievably high standards but He also provides the power by which you can attain to it. You *can* reduce your weight. You *can* embark on a programme of exercise. With Paul, you must say: 'I can do all things through Christ which strengtheneth me' (Philippians 4:13).

Fifthly, *start changing the way you behave*. Earlier we talked about changing the way you think, but there is another major approach to mood elevation that is tremendously effective – changing the way you act. Changing your thoughts is extremely important, but it takes a while before you begin to experience positive results. With this method, however – changing the way you behave – the results are almost immediate. Dr E. Stanley Jones says, 'It is easier to act yourself into a new way of thinking than to think yourself into a new way of acting.' Notice, he did not say it is more important, but *easier*. So if changing your thoughts might be a little too much for you at the moment, then start by changing your behaviour.

I once asked a depressed person to describe to me exactly what he did during the first hours of a day. This is what he said. 'I wake up, look at the clock, and whatever time it is, I pull the bedclothes over my head and try to go back to sleep. If I can't, I get up, go downstairs in my dressing gown, have a cup of tea and a piece of toast and read the morning paper. After I have read the paper, I go to the bathroom and have a wash and a shave. Then I pick up the paper again and read all the bits I missed in my first reading. After that, I might go out into the

51

garden, potter about in the shed, come back into the house and make myself a cup of tea, then pick up the paper again.' I said to my friend, 'If I was to do that I, too, would be depressed. You see, it's not only what you are thinking but what you are doing that is contributing to your depression.' In fact, two major questions which I ask all counsellees who come to me concerning the problem of depression, are these: 'What are you thinking that is making you depressed?' and 'What are you doing that is making you depressed?' The way we think and the way we act are contributing factors to depression. There's only one problem – when you are depressed, you don't feel like doing much to change the way you act or behave. This is where you are going to have to send up a quick telegramatic prayer to the Lord Jesus Christ and say, 'Lord, I know you will do your part – now help me to do my part.' Recognise that as a committed Christian you have a responsibility to live out the life Christ has given you, and acceptance of this responsibility is the step you now need to take. As a responsible person, God now asks you to do whatever He requires you to do *whether you feel like it or not*. I promise you that if you begin to do the things you know you should do, even though you don't feel like it, you will have taken the greatest and the most positive step to overcoming your depression. The key is not to follow your own feelings, but commit yourself to do what God wants you to do whether you feel like it or not. If you wait until you feel like it, you will never iron that pile of clothes, mark those papers, clean the house or mow the lawn. So make a list right now of the things you know it is your responsibility to complete. Get to work doing them in order to please God and those who are depending on you (wife, husband, children, boss, friends, etc.). Keep at it no matter how you feel, for I promise you as you work on changing your behaviour, God will work on changing your feelings. I have never known any counsellee I have ever counselled, suffering with depression who did not report a major change in their life when they began to attend to their responsibilities and do what they knew they should whether they felt like it or not.

Those who might find it difficult, because of deep depression, to plan or organise their day, should use the *Daily Activity Chart* – a simple tool used by counsellors to get their counsellees to plan the day that lies ahead. The chart consists of two sections. In the first column, marked Prospective, write out an hour by hour plan for what you would like to accomplish tomorrow. It may be that you will only carry out a part of the day's activities that you planned, but don't let that upset you. The simple act of beginning a plan of this kind will be greatly beneficial. Your plans need not be elaborate. Just put in one or two words in each section to indicate what you would like to do such as 'dress', 'have breakfast', 'write a letter', 'walk to the park' and so on. At the end of the day, record in the second section what you actually did during the hours of the day. This may be the same or different from what you had planned, but even if it was just staring at the television, put it down. In addition, label each activity with the letters V or P. V is for

Victory, P is for Pleasure. Victory activities are those which represent some accomplishment such as cooking a meal, doing the ironing, washing the dishes, driving to work. Pleasure activities might include reading a book, eating a meal, visiting a friend, etc. After you have written a V or a P for each activity, calculate the amount of pleasure or the degree of difficulty you experienced by scoring yourself on a scale of 0 to 5. For example, if you found no difficulty in getting dressed, you might decide to give yourself a V-1. If it was very difficult, you might give it a V-4. You can rate the pleasure activities in the same way. If reading a book brought you a good deal of pleasure, you might want to rate it P-4. If it didn't, you might rate it P-1.

A simple chart like this will help you get on with the task of living. It will cut down your tendency to debate with yourself endlessly about the value of various activities, and it will give you a sense of satisfaction that you are beginning to take things under control. Above all, it will disprove the erroneous belief that you are incapable of functioning effectively. Keep this Daily Activity Chart for at least a week. I will be surprised if you don't find a remarkable change in mood elevation after the first week.

Sixthly, *do something nice for others at least once a week*, especially someone in greater need than yourself. A friend of mine who is a minister in a large church in the city of Atlanta, Georgia, USA, once told me that he had in his church a man who for several months had been deeply depressed. One

| | LOOKING AHEAD | LOOKING BACK |
| | | |

LOOKING AHEAD
Plan your activities on an hour by hour basis either the night before or at the start of the day.

LOOKING BACK
At the end of the day, record what you actually did and rate each activity with a V or a P*

Date: _____

Time		
8–9		
9–10		
10–11		
11–12		
12–1		
1–2		
2–3		
3–4		
4–5		
5–6		
6–7		
7–8		
8–9		
9–12		

*Victory and Pleasure activities must be rated from 0–5. The higher the number the greater the sense of satisfaction.

morning as the man sat in the church office pouring out his troubles to my minister friend, he said to him, 'Look, I am due to be at the hospital in 15 minutes to visit a number of people who are desperately ill. Get your coat and come with me. We can talk on the way.' The man accompanied my friend to the hospital, and went inside with him to visit in all about 20 people who were suffering from some extremely distressing sicknesses, ranging from brain tumours to leukaemia. At the end of the morning, just as they were leaving the hospital, the man suddenly threw back his shoulders, drew himself up to his full height and said, 'Give me the names of those people once again, and I am going to visit them every day for as long as I can.' My friend was rather taken aback by his remarks and cautiously suggested that as he was depressed it would not be right to inflict his burden upon others. 'Wait a while,' he said, 'and when you are over your depression, we can talk about it further.' 'Depression,' said the man with a smile, 'what depression?' In just a matter of hours this man who had been suffering from depression for a number of months was suddenly set free. And why? Because he found that taking an interest in people who were less fortunate than himself was the key to this dissolving of his own problems. Karl Menninger, a famous psychiatrist, is reported to have told a conference of psychiatrists, 'One of the best remedies for depression is to get your patient to go to the other end of town, find a down-and-out, and do something nice for him.' In many of today's hospitals, occupational therapy has become an important aspect of the treatment of clinical depression. Doctors have found that keeping a patient occupied and interested in doing something creative often hastens recovery. I am always intrigued by a statement in the Bible concerning God's servant Job which reads thus: 'And the Lord turned the captivity of Job, when he *prayed for his friends*: also the Lord gave Job twice as much as he had before' (Job 42:10, italics mine). It seems that the turning point in Job's dire circumstances came when he turned from self-centred praying (i.e. focusing entirely on his own condition) and looked beyond his own needs to those of his friends.

You may be responding at this moment by saying to yourself: 'This all sounds fine, but how can I help anyone in the state I'm in?' Well, nothing can change you from the state you are in more effectively than doing something for someone who is in difficulty. When a person with a headache attends to someone with cancer, it's amazing how insignificant the headache seems. The Bible says: 'Whoever finds his life will lose it, and whoever loses his life for my sake will find it' (Matthew 10:39, NIV). When we focus only on ourselves, we lose ourselves. When we focus on others, we find ourselves. When you work on loving others rather than trying to get others to love you, your own needs will be met in a manner that will amaze you.

Seventhly, *give at least five minutes each day to the task of focusing on the fact of how much God loves you*. Over the years I have spent as a minister and a counsellor, I can't begin to count the number of times that people have said to me, 'You see, my problem is that I don't love the Lord enough. What can I do to develop a greater love for Him?' I have one stock answer for that question which I have given to a countless number of counsellees down the years. It is this – 'Your problem is not learning to love God more. *Your problem is that you don't know how much God loves you.*' Those who go about trying to work up a love for Jesus Christ usually finish up downcast and disillusioned, for our love for Him is but the response to His love for us. What do I mean? John the apostle puts the truth in these words: 'We love him, *because* he first loved us' (1 John 4:19). The great philosopher, Blaise Pascal, said, 'If everyone could see how much God loved them there would be no such thing as a sinner on the face of the earth.' Many of the problems in the lives of Christians stem from this fact that they don't realise how much they are *loved*. This is why we must come again and again to the foot of the Cross, for that is the central place from which the revelation of God's love flows. There the heart of God is unveiled. It is the place of supreme revelation. Gazing at the Cross, a number of things happen to us. We see our Lord's burning love for lost sinners, for you and for me. We become conscious that divine love is a love that is unconditional. We are not loved if we do this or that – but loved for ourselves alone. Nothing in us gave rise to it; nothing in us can quench it. It is love without condition and without end. When we focus upon the fact that God loves us, and we perceive it, even feebly, for what it is, then, in the depth of our being, a similar love is generated. It is not the fruit of labour, nor the effort of the flesh. The scales fall from our eyes. Seeing His love, our own love flames in response. We love *because*. To help counsellees absorb this truth of God's love for them being the motivating force of their love for Him, I use an intriguing paraphrase of 1 Corinthians 13 which was originally prepared by a Christian counsellor in California, Dick Dickinson. This particular paraphrase has been extremely helpful to hundreds of depressed people, and has brought many into a new understanding of God's love for them.

Because God loves me He is slow to lose patience with me.

Because God loves me he takes the circumstances of my life and uses them in a constructive way for my growth.

Because God loves me He does not treat me as an object to be possessed and manipulated.

Because God loves me He has no need to impress me with how great and powerful He is, because HE IS GOD, nor does He belittle me as His child in order to show me how important He is.

Because God loves me He is for me. He wants to see me mature and develop in His love.

Because God loves me He does not send down his wrath on every little mistake I make, of which there have been many.

Because God loves me he does not keep score of all my sins and then beat me over the head with them whenever he gets the chance.

Because God loves me He is deeply grieved when I do not walk in the ways that please Him, because He sees this as evidence that I don't trust

Him and love Him as I should.

Because God loves me He rejoices when I experience His power and strength and stand up under the pressures of life for His Name's sake.

Because God loves me He keeps on working patiently with me even when I feel like giving up, and can't see why he doesn't give up with me too.

Because God loves me He keeps on trusting me when at times I don't even trust myself.

Because God loves me He never says, 'There's no hope for you.' Rather He patiently works with me, loves me and disciplines me in such a way that it is hard for me to understand the depth of His concern for me.

Because God loves me He never forsakes me even though many of my friends might.

Because God loves me He stands with me when I have reached the rock bottom of despair: when I see the real me and compare that with his righteousness, holiness, beauty and love. It is at a moment like this that I can really believe that God loves me. Yes, the greatest of all gifts is God's perfect love!

Focus on this paraphrase every day until the awareness of God's love for you begins to fill your heart. Read it to yourself out loud. There will be times when you don't believe that God loves you, but try and imagine how you would read it if you were utterly and fully convinced of it. Then read it like that. I have mentioned before that you sometimes have to act yourself into a new way of thinking, and a number of research studies on the subject of depression support this idea. So throw back your shoulders, lift up your voice and read the words each morning out loud with emphasis. Ponder each sentence and let the wonder of each statement penetrate deep into your soul. I promise you that although nothing might happen at first, after a while the truth contained in this passage will take effect.

God bless you as you take the steps necessary to overcoming your depression.